CEREMONIES OF THE RED ROAD:
How to Become a True Human Being

Lynn Manyfires

ACKNOWLEDGEMENTS

To my beloved editor, Carol Rawlins, for bringing out the best in my words and honoring my feelings.

To my Mother, Freida Newman, who always bugged me by telling me 'You should write a book!" I always brushed it away, thinking she didn't know me very well.

To all of my friends, blog readers and fans for allowing me to share my thoughts and remember how much the spiritual ways meant to me.

To Tom Owen-Towle for his constant and continuous encouragement to finish my book. Without his gentle but determined nudging, I don't think this book would have ever been finished and I thank him for his heartening encouragement.

To my *hunka* brother of the Hawk nation, Wade Helms, my love, gratitude and deepest respect. He was always there for me, especially during the dark times. He never let me fall or allowed me to give up and several times, saved me. When I wandered in a spiritual desert, hungry for some kind of connection, he was there for me. In all ways, he is truly a brother of my heart and my spirit.

Last, but certainly not least, to the Creator of All That Is for bringing me to the Red Road. I was guided, educated, humbled, shown the hope of a new way of life and in general, shown what life could be like when walking in a Sacred manner. Thus it was the Prayers and Ceremonies that saved me, shaped me and made me into a True Human Being, in spite of all of my imperfections.

CONTENTS

1 CEREMONIES

Wicho'an wakan (Sacred Ceremonies) have been a part of human existence for longer than we can truly know. The Latin word, *Caerimōnia,* describes them as reverent rites of sacredness and respect. Ceremonies bring us together to honor and observe a sacred occasion. They acknowledge the deeper truths of Life and teach us how to walk a path of Honor, Respect and Balance. Every act of a Ceremony reminds us that everything, and everyone, has a place in the order of the whole. And it is the Ceremonies that call out to our souls.

The Lakota/Dakota ceremonies I experienced not only taught me how to walk "in a Good Way" but they became stepping stones on my journey to something greater. While each of the Ceremonies could stand on its own, each seemed to build upon the previous, revealing more about my true spirit than what I could see.

Lessons came, not just in the performance of a Ceremony but even in the preparation. Holding the purpose of why I was performing a Ceremony helped to keep me focused on Spirit on a daily basis. Elders leading the Ceremonies would ask us to "see through" the deceptions and distractions of the outside world and to remember who we truly were…cherished Sons and Daughters of the Creator.

Many times over the years, a Ceremony would go awry or be delayed and sometimes had to be cancelled entirely. These delays and interruptions were considered normal and indeed Elders felt it was further proof of the Creator's design that we be true to our intentions. For a Ceremony without spirit, they said, was just a ritual.

Walking the path of the Red Road is not blindly following some religion. Instead, it is a 'Way of Life'...a lifelong journey, filled with many large and small lessons. The Ceremonies brought me closer to the Creator and more importantly...with my True Self.

For me, this path demanded I be worthy of the Spirit within. And that is what I hope I have done. I wrote this book to share how the Ceremonies sparked life into that Sacred part of me, opened up my heart and taught me wisdom. The Ceremonies of the Red Road have been a

3

blessed guide thru all the joys and desolations of my life. They unveiled my true self, united my Spirit with the Human part of me and allowed me to see my place in the whole. They taught me how to be a True Human Being.

2 THE BEGINNING

I was 12, sitting in a Southern Baptist church, listening to the minister ask if there was anyone to whom God had spoken and who would now accept Jesus Christ as their Savior.

It was a question I had heard many times, but this particular Sunday I suddenly became keenly aware of its significance. I asked myself 'Why hasn't God spoken to me? Doesn't He know I'm getting older? That I only have a few short years before people start wondering why I haven't been baptized?"

In that moment, I felt a sharp pang of fear. Maybe God knew there was something wrong with me…that I was a bad person and that was why He hadn't bothered to speak with me. My family had been telling me that I was bad. Perhaps this was a sign that it was true.

After that Sunday, I began to question others, discreetly, about God 'talking' to people but no one took my questions seriously. I became disillusioned and unsatisfied with what I was told. And what was more, I began noticing that their words didn't match their actions. I slipped away from my church, disheartened and unnoticed.

I became very disbelieving in the existence of God and the real purpose of life. I hid behind all those questions that others voiced: How could a supposedly loving God allow atrocities to occur? I told people that God didn't exist for me. I never shared the truth that I feared I wasn't a good enough for God. My despair walked with me for many years. Unknown to me, this was the beginning of my spiritual quest.

In the beginning, that quest took an unusual form. It started with how I selected my dating companions in high school. I chose them, not for looks (well, maybe just a little, after all, I was 14), not for who they were at school but for their religion...especially, if it was a religion that was new to me. I told everyone that it was only curiosity...but it was always more than that.

I spent a heavenly year (no pun intended) with a sweet Catholic boy. With the Catholic faith, I found ethereal churches filled with incense and candles and a wonderful intuitiveness for making one feel that God truly was there. They also had unfortunate tendency towards repeating litanies and what I like to refer to as the "stand-up, sit-down, kneel-down" syndrome. It seemed as if the people served the religion instead of the religion serving the people. It gave them structure while allowing them to live with God without putting much effort into it. But the religion did spark a sympathetic chord within me...at least with regards to guilt. I almost married that sweet person, not for himself, but for his beliefs.

The Catholic boy was followed by a nice Jewish boy. I was attracted to Judaism because of the mystery of their rituals, a strong sense of connectedness and the option (at least on the part of the men) to argue and discuss their opinions on what God intended in any particular verse of the Torah without being ostracized or ridiculed for it. I loved the integration of intellect with faith. Even then, I displayed a tendency to favor logic in faith. However, I did not care for the hint of discrimination I felt when I would not convert to their faith. I did not like that women were relegated to a position of inequality. This, along with the feeling that this religion did not serve my needs caused me to move on. I wasn't sure what I wanted but I started to know what I didn't want.

Finally... the man of my dreams! Only he, too, was searching. Hinduism, Buddhism, Taoism, Zen (mostly Eastern religions). None of these religions spoke to my heart but they spoke to him. We had intense spiritual discussions exploring the truths of these various faiths; each crystallizing our own belief system. He moved from one faith to another, read mightily on each and then shared his absolute certainty that here was finally the true religion. He was very devoted to finding his faith and ignited a ravenous curiosity in me. But he was very strong in his opinions. I was forced to become stronger in mine. He demanded that I defend my ideas, justifying them with slow and careful thought. Many times, I couldn't rationalize my reasoning for often it was based on some innate feeling of truth, not reason. This was a long, spiritually enriching chapter in my life. And as the pendulum started to swing back, I began to leave behind the guilt I'd always felt.

I began to *choose* which beliefs were mine and which were ones I had adopted but did not truly believe. I had been building the core all along and I became aware of how defined the structure was. I was forging and fashioning the true form and content of who I was spiritually.

At SDSU in 1985, I came upon a path that would weave a tighter fabric of my soul. It was there that my interest in Native Americans was renewed. I say renewed because I was a hippie who dressed in Native beaded headbands, wore moccasins and braids. It became a common theme in my life...this special affinity with Natives. Indeed, my first job was at a plant in my home town that was staffed almost entirely by Apaches, Arapahos, Winnebago, Navajos and Cherokee. I laughed with glee at their wicked sense of humor and they taught me some of their finest cuss words.

Chance (or destiny) brought me to a professor at SDSU who whetted my appetite for knowledge regarding local tribes. This professor was also employed by the tribes to make determinations regarding the sacredness of remains at construction sites. He introduced me to the local Native tribes who called themselves the Kumeyaay. Their history was not what I had read in the books: Eating shellfish from Mission Bay, leeching acorns in Torrey Pines, hunting for food in the Laguna's, dying in Mission Valley...right where apartment and professional buildings had been built.

I became more involved in my Native American studies and less in my Business major. My everyday focus changed. The intent and sole purpose of my life became to absorb and TOTALLY understand the Native Culture!! I took a Native Law class where I learned perhaps more than I wished to about how lawmakers and politicians had cheated Natives out of their destiny and their human rights. A class on 'Stories and Traditions' taught me that no matter how they were portrayed in non-Native history, they were a learned and sacred people. They were human beings who had reacted much as any culture would have if others tried to take their Land, their way of Life, their Children, their Dignity and their Faith.

For awhile I convinced myself that my search was only my 'usual curiosity' into religions. But soon even I had to admit that my single-minded fixation into anything Native was something much, MUCH more!

I became obsessed with Native art but as a poor college student, I simply couldn't afford the price tag on most pieces. But I simply HAD to have them! For the first time in my life, some inner sense of 'knowing' said "you can make these." And so I did.

Eventually, in the process of learning to make these various Native items, the most important step in my spiritual evolution came. I began to ask WHY they were made? That question into the meaning of why the items were created would ultimately be the catalyst to transform me.

As I began to explore the ritual aspects of tribal life, I began to make connections with the local tribes. Once I began to attend their ceremonies, I began to feel fulfilled at a deeper level and nothing, not even my studies, mattered.

And so it was that my "obsession" would reveal not only my own ancestry but would bring me to my true spiritual path...that which would reveal my true self…the path of the "Red Road."

3 FIRST INIPI (SWEAT LODGE)

The very first ceremony I was honored to attend was an *Inipi* (commonly known as a sweat lodge) held on the Manzanita reservation (commonly referred to as the 'rez') in San Diego. The Kumeyaay, like so many tribes, had begun the process of re-connecting spiritually. Many tribes found that the years of being forbidden to hold their ceremonies had caused them to lose many of their traditions. Like many tribes, they found themselves following the Lakota/Dakota spiritual customs. The Kumeyaay found the ceremony a powerful way to make a spiritual connection with the Creator.

It was so powerful that many Native recovery centers were utilizing the sweat lodge as part of a recovery plan. During this time, many were searching for a spiritual connection...so were many non-Natives. The sweat lodge ceremony offered not only Purification on a physical level but on an emotional and spiritual level. For me, it provided the foundation for walking the Red Road.

By the time of my first sweat lodge, I had graduated from college and was working for a large company. Once I left college, I lost contact with many in the local tribal community. My daughter moved in with her boyfriend and suddenly I was experiencing loss on all levels...the loss of my identity as a Mother...the loss of being a vibrant and inquisitive Student...and the loss of spiritual connections. In fact, while I was thriving financially for the first time in many years, my life felt hollow and without purpose.

Having passed thru the time of obsession with "all things Native", I had begun a more quiet and solitary connection with the Creator, but I was hungry for more. I turned my attention once again to ceremonial items and the meaning behind them. I wanted...no NEEDED...to make them.

I decided to start simply with making a medicine bag for myself. I visited a local Tandy leather store to pick up some supplies and there I met a woman who would become my first mentor on the Red Road. She was working in the store and while she helped me find what I needed, she quietly slipped in some very penetrating questions. And that is how my relationship with Nekasowa (Neka) began. I would discover later that she was known, in both the California and Arizona tribal communities, for her work in the prisons teaching the Lakota spiritual ways. After a month of regular visits to the store, I was invited by Neka to attend her weekly Drum circle.

That visit was the beginning of my sisterhood with Neka. She taught me so much about Native teachings. She helped me make my first drum with an Elk hide, a drum with the clearest 'call' I was ever to have. Not only did I learn to make ceremonial items in a traditional manner but I learned about the various ceremonies.

I had known Neka for almost a year when she invited me to attend a sweat lodge on the Manzanita rez. I was excited and honored to be invited because many lodges at the time were by invitation only. I peppered her with questions but she told me very little about the ceremony. Being a confidant woman for the most part, I was unexpectedly worried that I would say or do something that would offend, and I shared this concern with her. Still, she said nothing.

There was just one obstacle – getting to the rez. Neka's truck had been demolished in a major collision on the rez and my disintegrating vehicle simply could not make it up to the mountains. Frantic that I might miss what might be my only opportunity to attend a sweat lodge, I started considering things I never had before. Despite having absolutely no credit or the $300 deposit, somehow I was able to rent a car. It seemed like a miracle…almost as if I was' meant' to attend this ceremony. Neka felt my single-minded determination to attend demonstrated serious intention.

The night of the sweat lodge came and I was filled with nervous energy. I was still worried and utterly frustrated with Neka for leading me blindly into a situation fraught with taboos. I would learn afterward that it had been a test to see how I would act. Would I behave as a thoughtless non-Native or would I act with honor and respect? After dropping off the food for the pot luck feast afterward, we headed down the hill to the lodge.

It was nearly dark but I could still see that the area was divided into 3 parts or 'circles': the lodge; the altar and the pit where the rocks were placed with wood on top.

Two men known as 'Fire Tenders' tended and cared for the fire. Once the sacred fire was lit, no one could cross the 'sacred path', an invisible line that led from the fire to the altar to the lodge. Many people quietly chatted or made Prayer Ties (colored squares of yellow, white, black and red filled with tobacco that held their prayers to hang in the lodge). The men wore shorts and T-shirts while the women wore full-length cotton dresses or long skirts with T-shirts. The altar held various leather pouches and stones and other items but most notable were the buffalo skull on the ground and a *Čhaŋnúŋpa* (pipe) leaning against a horizontal stick supported by 2 others.

Neka left me to myself and I listened to the crackling and popping of the fire as it grew colder. I heard many conversations…some congenial…some ceremonial. Some people shared the various ceremonies and differences they had encountered on each rez. When it was apparent that the *Inyan* (rocks) were ready, the people began to either change clothes or remove the outer layer, including all jewelry.

The sweat lodge leader came to the center and spoke about how we would line up around the outside of the lodge, how to enter and where we were to sit once inside. He reminded us to show respect by being quiet when the rocks were first brought in. I was told later that the water pourer could be a Holy One but more often the lodge was run by an *Ikčé Wičháša / Ikčé Wíŋyaŋ* (Common Man/Common Woman). As people started to line up, I looked around for Neka but she was nowhere to be seen. My panic began in earnest. Had she left me to go into this alone with no idea of what would happen? My anger and resentment were tinged with fear.

I followed the actions of the woman in front of me as we came around the back of the lodge in a clockwise direction and stood before the door. The lodge was approximately 4 ft tall with a small door about 3 ft tall. The woman in front of me came to the door, looked up to Creator and then turned clockwise, honoring each direction before finally getting down on her hands and knees and gently touching her head to the ground to honor Mother Earth while saying *Ho, Mitákuye Oyásiŋ* (We Are all Related). I followed, full of fear, worry and nervous excitement. This was about to get more real than I had ever dreamed.

Coming into the dark of the lodge on my hands and knees, I could make out that the one who poured the water was sitting to the right of the door with his wife just behind him. He pointed to where he wanted me to sit, next to a

Grandfather who kept his eyes down and did not speak. Finally, Neka entered and sat opposite from me, smiling a big smile at me. I did not return her smile, instead looking away.

The sweat lodge leader began to share what the 4 'doors' of the lodge meant. A 'door' (or round) commonly consisted of a teaching, 3-4 sacred songs, Prayers and finally a calling for the flap to be lifted so the cool air might come in. The first round was to Purify and shed our human-ness. The second was to Pray. The third was to listen for the Answer to our prayers. And the 4th was to thank the Creator for hearing our prayers…for guiding us…and for bringing that which we needed. At the end of the 4th song, we would yell out as one "*Ho Mitákuye Oyásiŋ*" and the Fire Tender would open the door as quickly as possible.

Many teachings were given that night about what is expected of one who follows the path of the Red Road. He spoke of how these ways are different than others and how important it is to come into the lodge to purify, to speak with the Creator, to have an open heart...and to be willing to be guided. Looking at each of us, he stated that it was no accident that each of us was there...that we were right where we were supposed to be...where the Creator needed us to be. He told us that there would be Sacred songs to call in the Spirits to help us. [These were Spiritual Beings who came to the leader on his vision quest and promised to help him throughout his life]

By this time, I was experiencing claustrophobia from being in the dark in such a small place with too many people. Fear was starting to fill me and I wanted desperately to leave. I was about to ask when all of a sudden, the Fire Tender brought in the first 7 rocks. Cedar was sprinkled on each of the rocks and smoke filled the small space. "This is medicine," he said, "breathe it in." Someone passed around some fresh white sage and told us that when it became difficult for us to breathe to hold it to our noses and take in the smell of the sage deep into our lungs. More medicine, we were told.

As each rock was brought in, the leader used the antlers of a deer to place the rocks into the four directions of the pit with the last 3 on top of the others. [The Elders would later tell me that the antlers of the Deer were used to represent The People aligning themselves with the Creator in obedience...for deer always placed their back hooves in the tracks of their front hooves...leaving only one set of tracks.]

Finally, the rocks were all in and the leader began to share another teaching. I became aware of the heat building from the rocks. And yet, his words held me and I began to experience a sense of the lodge being 'filled up' with something. Is this how one met Creator? I was thrilled and petrified at the same time. Finally, he asked for the pail of water and the door closed.

In a short period of time, the lodge became a place full of heat and the unknown. In the dark I heard the sound of water being gently poured over the rocks and steam hissing off of them. More water was poured and again the rocks hissed. I was gently sweating and I thought to myself "I think I'll be okay."

As the leader continued to pour more and more water on the rocks, he called for a song. The song was so gentle, so prayerful that it carried me away to another time. I did not feel the heat and I felt myself gently rocking to the song as the sweat from my brow dropped gently onto the ground. Every part of me wanted to sing that song. I felt an embracing sense of sacredness fill my spirit and I *needed* to lift my voice to the Creator...as if to say "I have heard your 'call'...I am here". The other songs, which did not carry that same prayerful feel, did not hold my attention.

Once again, I became aware of the discomfort of the heat. My hips hurt from sitting on the hard ground and my dress, sopped with sweat, clung to me uncomfortably. Just as the desire to leave surged again, I was startled to hear *Ho Mitákuye Oyásiŋ* and the flap lifted immediately.

The steam flowed out of the lodge like fog coming in off the ocean. People wiped their brows and gulped in the cool night air. Many lay down. I could see Neka's head turned towards me but I could not see the look on her face. The Grandfather seated next to me was very still. I had a vague remembrance of him softly singing a few of the songs but for the most part, he had not spoken or moved.

The leader began to speak of some of the older traditions of the lodge as he dipped the gourd into the water and passed it around to each person in the lodge [Some lodges offer water between rounds while others do not].

He told us that, in the old days men wore a rope around their ankles that led outside the lodge for the Fire Tenders to grab hold of, if needed. For it was said that sometimes the spirit would leave the body and get lost and could not find the body to return to. That *HAD* to be a superstitious story, I thought to myself. "Nowadays", he said, "I ask you to watch over each other to ensure that all return."

The sweat lodge leader reminded us that the next round was for our Prayers and encouraged us to pray not only for our Family and Friends but for the Elders and the Children…our Communities…our Leaders…for All our Relatives…for Mother Earth…and for ourselves. When everyone had drunk their fill, he called to the Fire Tender to bring in the next 7 rocks. I thought on what he had asked us to pray for. I had never heard of praying for everyone and everything and certainly never for myself. As the flap came down for the 2nd round, I began to experience a 'spiritual shift'.

As the dark wrapped around us, I heard the gourd being dipped into the water and slowly poured over the rocks. He asked each of us to speak our Prayers aloud because the spoken word holds great power. I panicked not only because the steam felt much hotter this time but because I had never said my prayers aloud…having been taught that prayers were private between you and the Creator. I worried that the people would laugh at me, finding my prayers silly or foolish.

That's when the first brother spoke. I could dimly see that he had gotten on his knees and was bent in a prayerful position. He began by humbly thanking the Creator for everything in his life. He asked for prayers for certain people around him. I began to feel uncomfortable listening to what felt like very private thoughts, and I tried to focus my thoughts instead on what it was I wanted to pray for. It had never occurred to me driving up the hill that I would need to be conscious of what I would pray for. I'd always been spontaneous in my prayers. Whatever came to my mind was what I prayed for. I wondered if they would consider me a shallow person when they heard my prayers.

Suddenly, the brother's words caught my attention. The words seemed louder and clearer than the rest, yet in reality, he was speaking quietly. He was gently asking for his brother's forgiveness [his brother was in the lodge]. The lodge became still as he began to share that he had spoken badly of his brother behind his back and that he deeply regretted causing him any harm. He prayed that he might make amends and that they may once again grow close as they had been in their youth. After he had finished, many in the lodge said, "*Aho*" (similar to an 'Amen') or *"Philámayaye"* (Thank you) in response. I found his prayer humbling and I admired his courage in openly sharing what he had done. Could I ever have that kind of courage? As each person, in turn, shared their prayers aloud, my respect and humility grew.

When it came time for my prayers, I was still nervous but I knew I had to honor their bravery by opening my heart and speaking truly. Haltingly and with a lot of fear, I spoke my pitiful prayers aloud and was grateful to hear many say *"Aho"* or *"Philámayaye"* at the end. During the entire time I had prayed, I had barely noticed the heat. Suddenly, it was uncomfortably hot and it felt like an eternity while 4 songs were sung. I struggled not to ask to leave and just when I could take no more, the door was called with my voice being the loudest!

Dropping all pretense of strength, I immediately sank to the ground. I had started to feel light-headed and not fully in my own body at the end of the 2nd round and I eagerly drank an entire gourd full of water…twice.

The leader, giving us all time to cool down, shared more teachings. He reminded us that the 3rd round was to receive the Answers from the Creator to our prayers. He encouraged us not to judge what came…to simply trust and accept whatever made itself known to us…whether it be a vision or spoken words. Even a feeling in our hearts/spirits could be the answer we sought. He then called for the next 7 rocks and I groaned inside. I wasn't sure I could make it. Once the rocks were in, everyone sat up. I noticed that several took their towels and wrapped it over their heads like a shawl and I decided it was wise to do so as well. The flap came down and darkness filled the lodge again.

The 3rd round started out ferociously, like a blast from Hades. The leader called for a song, all the while pouring gourd after gourd of water on the rocks. When the people started to sing, many sang in broken breaths, gasping from the heat. I could not see the red hot rocks for all the steam. And still he poured more and more water. The towel around my head did not help prevent the steam from burning my lungs and I covered my entire face. I was really suffering now and I just wanted to get out of this hell.

It was about that time, that the Grandfather next to me spoke in my ear. With gentle Compassion in his voice, he whispered that when the heat became more than I could bear, to lie down upon Mother Earth, for that was where the cool air was, and that Mother would show mercy to one whose prayers were true. His last words were "When it gets hot," he said "Pray harder."

Immediately, I laid down on the earth and felt the coolness he spoke of. Distantly, I heard the 'voice' of the rocks as more and more water was poured upon them. Even on the ground there was still great heat and so I began to pray...harder. I spoke of hearing Creator's call and that despite my fears, I had come. I 'whined' about having to suffer just to hear Him. What was wrong with me that I was unable to find a spiritual community? And why, oh why, did these ways call to the deepest part of my soul? Where was I to go from here? Finally, with tears streaming down into Mother, I surrendered and asked for the answers that Creator would have me know.

I had been praying so hard that I hadn't even been aware of the songs or the call for the door until suddenly a great light shone in and I saw the steam struggling to leave the small doorway. When I finally could see through the steam, I saw everyone laying on the ground gasping for air…including the leader. The Grandfather's words were true. While my senses told me that there had been great heat, my prayers had lessened my awareness of it, and hence, my suffering.

After a time of quiet, as the steam left the lodge, people slowly began to sit up. The leader was the first. He just sat there quietly as his wife joined him. I could see that Neka had sat up but was bent deeply forward. We two-leggeds, with all our wisdom and intellect, had been taken down to the ground. There was a great sense of equality in that moment. Before the Creator, we were all equal…we were all the same. And what united us in that moment was our devotion to following the Creator.

As if reading my mind, the leader spoke about not judging our fellow human beings. 'It is said that it is unwise to judge another for one cannot know what the Creator has asked of them', he said. The lodge was completely still…even the rocks were silent. I could 'feel' that everyone was listening with their whole hearts. And I wondered if I could ever refrain from thinking negative thoughts about another. And then the thought came 'perhaps…if I followed these ways'. The leader spoke a few moments more and then called for the last 7 rocks. The Fire Tender brought in the remaining rocks and joined us, pulling the flap down and the darkness descended for the 4th round.

The leader did not speak for some time…nor did he pour any water…letting the rocks 'speak' for him. They seemed to reach out and 'touch' each of us for one last time. When he did speak, it was to say we needed to honor these rocks who had sacrificed their lives for us two-leggeds. He emphasized that their sacrifice had been necessary for our purification that we might pray with the Creator in a clear and sacred way.

He then spoke of how important the value of Sacrifice was in Lakota ways…that all Relatives sacrificed for each other…the four-legged and plant nations gave of their lives that we were fed and thereby lived…and he conveyed to us how truly important our sacrifices were for our Families, Friends and Communities. He told us that it wasn't a matter of *if* our prayers had been heard…for they had been. But two-leggeds especially, he declared, needed to purify to come into that Holy space in order to remember that they were truly the Sons and Daughters of the Creator.

And as he was speaking, I looked deeply into the rocks…a place I had looked many times during this lodge. Where before they had been a reminder of heat; now I saw the rocks with new eyes. I now saw them as living Relatives and I felt my gratitude grow…just as the leader reminded us that our focus of the 4th door was that of Gratitude.

The leader stopped speaking and called for a song. I heard Neka's voice begin to sing a pure, sweet prayer song. I heard the sound of water being poured very slowly upon the rocks. As the steam gently rose, so too did the song, filling the lodge with loving gratitude. I felt my spirit embrace this gentle shift. Tears ran from my eyes as I joined them to sing the chorus. I began to rock in time to the beat of the drum…humility filling me.

And then in a swift moment, I was floating above my body, watching the brothers and sisters sing. I didn't feel surprised or frightened. In fact, it felt like the most natural thing in the world. And then I started to move towards somewhere. There was no sense of time…just a sense that I was moving 'Up'. It felt so good…so free.

Suddenly, there was a sensation of being grabbed firmly by the foot and I felt 'pulled' down. There was a jolt and I heard myself say 'Ooof'. I opened my eyes to find a hand on my shoulder shaking me. I felt irritation. I hadn't wanted to come back. I blinked in the low light to see that the flap to the lodge was open and that the others were leaving. To this day, I do not remember where I went or how I lost that time but it does not puzzle me. I have thought many times that perhaps I was being brought to a place where the Elders/Spirits could speak with me.

I look back now to that first sweat lodge and see the synchronicity moving through my life during those times. All seemed designed to illuminate my search and lead me to the real truths…confirming the Light…the Love.

As I dropped into sleep that night, utterly exhausted, satisfaction washed over me followed by a great spiritual hunger.

I wanted more!

4 ČHAŊNÚŊPA WAKAN
(PIPE CEREMONY)

The *Čhaŋnúŋpa* (Pipe) Ceremony is one Lakota ceremony that can be performed not only in a group but in solitude as well.

My first exposure to the Pipe came from my mentor and friend, Neka. She was introducing me to more of the ways, and we did a small Pipe ceremony together. Truthfully, I don't remember much because I was doing the non-Native thing by trying to remember the technical requirements instead of 'feeling' the spirit of the ceremony. I think she was frustrated with me for she did something that I was later to learn was unusual...she lent me her

Pipe to do a ceremony on my own at home. I was honored and so I tried to be ultra careful with her Pipe but I still managed to lose a small piece of red felt she needed for the Pipe. It simply and mysteriously disappeared. I was so sorry to be unable to keep my word and return it exactly as given to me. And she was angry with me for awhile over that. While it might not have been the most auspicious beginning of my relationship to the Pipe, it opened another door into the world of Spirit

The second time I participated in a Pipe Ceremony came at the end of a sweat lodge. Gathered in a circle around the altar…sweaty, drained and feeling like babes just born…we were told that the melding of stone and wood represented the union of Earth and Spirit…that the Pipe was loaded with a mixture of tobacco, red willow bark, sage and other sacred herbs…that we were to hold the bowl with our left hand (considered to be sacred by many indigenous peoples). To demonstrate the inter-connectedness of all, each of us would light the Pipe for another. Finally, we were told what it meant to pray with the Pipe. Many of us already knew the story of the White Buffalo Calf Woman and how she brought the original White Buffalo Calf Pipe. The Pipe resides on the Green River Rez in the care of its 19th caretaker, Arvol Lookinghorse, a *Wičháša Wakȟáŋ* (Holy Man). For many of us, the very mention of his name reminded us of the sacredness of the Pipe ceremony before us. And it was there that I heard (for the first of many times) that it is said that "whatever you pray for with the Pipe will come true".

With the embers of the fire burning low and the darkness enfolding us, the *Cannunpa Yuha*

(Pipe Carrier) offered a traditional Pipe song while the Pipe was being filled, followed by some words in prayer. After that, the Pipe was passed to each of us in order to place our prayers into the tobacco. Finally, the Pipe was lit and passed around once again to each of us to 'send' our prayers heavenwards on the winds.

I felt a great sense of honor and humility as I received the Pipe to offer my Prayers. I had seen a few of the more experienced people hold the bowl against their heart with the stem facing heavenwards as they prayed and I felt the need to do the same. As I did so, a bolt of energy hit my heart. Dazed and swaying a bit, I finished my prayers and passed the Pipe on, wondering what had just happened. Some spoke their prayers aloud but most spoke their prayers silently and soon the Pipe returned to me, lit.

I had not been told that one did not inhale the smoke from the Pipe but instead gently puffed at it. Being a smoker at the time, I inhaled deeply and started coughing uncontrollably. A few people smiled my way. Irreverently in the moment, I thought of what my Yankton brothers had told me: that since the White Man had been kind enough to give them whiskey (which ruined many lives), that they had simply returned the favor by giving the White Nation tobacco. I took 4 puffs and pointed the stem of the Pipe toward the 7 directions: Creator, Mother Earth, 4 directions and finally touching the stem to my heart and I passed it on.

Standing there, it seemed as if the night and all its relatives held its breath. No one spoke as they gazed thoughtfully into the fire. Someone took up a drum and started softly to sing some sacred songs. I felt as if time was slipping. A 'difference' settled in my soul, as if I didn't belong there but in another time. I stood that way – half in this world and half in the other – until the last song was sung and the Pipe was done.

All remained quiet as the Pipe Carrier respectfully broke down the Pipe and returned it to its leather casing. We stood in perfect silence, unwilling to break the spell of Spirit…and in that moment, there was a "oneness' between us…and I felt a Holiness.

Three years later, I would stand before Chief Richard Swallow in ceremony. He was presenting my Pipe to me and explaining what it meant to be a Pipe Carrier. He wanted me to know the seriousness of the commitment I was making. He told me that to be a Pipe Carrier was to live for the good of The People, to sacrifice for The People, to always try to Speak and Act in a Good Way, to do things when asked that we might not feel like doing. He told me that now my life would be lived for The People.

As he presented the Pipe to me three times, I felt a great weight of responsibility settle on my heart and my soul...almost as if I were 'taking vows' of a Nun. Suddenly, I found the commitments to be so heavy, so overwhelming that when the Pipe was offered the 3rd time, I could not accept the Pipe. I explained that I didn't know if I could make that commitment to be all those things. And so Chief Richard agreed to hold my Pipe for one year for me to consider if this was something I wanted to take on. I thought long and hard and had many conversations with Elders about it over that year. Some agreed with me that it was a heavy responsibility and counseled me not to do it. Others thought that since the Creator had guided me to it, He must have need of me to do so. By the end of that year, as I accepted that Pipe into my hands, I knew that I was dedicating a portion of my life to a way of living that demanded the highest Honor, Respect and Sacrifice.

5 YUWÍPI (HOUSE CEREMONY)

In the April of 1995, I joined with a group of spiritual brothers/sisters to bring Elders from many tribes together at the First Unitarian Universalist Church in San Diego to share their wisdom, traditions and teachings. 'The Gathering of Elders' brought together the likes of Russell Means, Wallace Black Elk, Floyd 'Red Crow' Westerman and many other well-known individuals to participate. They shared their stories, their perceptions and even the prophecies of where they thought the world was going.

The Gathering of Elders was a turning point in my life as it was there that I first met my Relatives from the Yankton rez, including the young man who was their current Intercessor of the Sun Dance. Being a complete novice in the traditional ways, I approached the Intercessor directly to ask him if he would be willing to give me my Native name and I presented him with tobacco. Startled and a little taken aback, he slowly agreed. And so that very summer, I traveled for the first time to the Yankton rez in South Dakota.

Because of my boldness in asking the Sun Dance Intercessor if he would honor me with my Native name, I arrived at the Yankton rez just prior to the Sun Dance. This was a time when they performed sacred ceremonies, including my naming ceremony. I was busily completing the last of my duties for my naming, when I was called, along with everyone else, to attend a *Yuwípi* - commonly called a 'House' Ceremony.

Walking into the house, I was amazed to see that all the furniture had been completely removed and that the windows had been blacked out and all the People sat on floor along the walls. I had been told that *Yuwípi* ceremonies were performed to ask the Spirits for help in finding lost objects or the cause of a sickness. The medicine man was bound and tied up in a sacred blanket and placed on a buffalo robe on the floor. It would be the spirits who would come and untie him. Often flickering lights might be seen. Some of the spirits that could come might be little people, fairies, stone spirits and animals. These spirits were said to be able to remove illnesses as well as answer questions.

A woman stood by the door and directed me to sit next to a woman I did not know. Looking around, I realized that there was no one I recognized. I felt nervous, having no idea what to expect. There was an air of anticipation in the air that didn't show on most of the faces around me. The smoke and smell of the white sage and cedar was thick and had an almost immediate calming effect on me. In the center of the room was a young man of about 11 years old seated on a chair. His mother sat on the floor next to him. I had seen them both around the rez a few times and came to know that he and his mother had traveled out from Mexico with the help of some generous individuals for a healing. The young man had been ill for some time and the doctors had been unable to diagnose his condition.

In the center of the room facing the boy was a buffalo rug with a small altar in front of it. Prayer ties, hanging on sinew string, were wrapped around 4 sticks representing the 4 directions. The boy looked nervous and his mother was continuously reassuring him while looking a bit anxious herself. I felt the excitement build even stronger, when one of the Intercessor's assistants abruptly stepped into the room. He began explaining that we were here to witness and pray. Then he described what would happen in the ceremony.

First, he said, the Intercessor would be brought in and seated within the prayer tie circle. Then he would call upon the Spirits that guided him not only to diagnose the condition of the young man but to bring a healing to him as well. We were admonished that no matter what we saw or heard, we were _not_ to touch the Intercessor or interfere in the ceremony in any way.

The assistant pulled back the curtain covering the doorway and the Intercessor and another assistant entered. The prayer tie fence was "opened" up and the Intercessor sat down in the middle of the rug. A drum was handed to him and he sang some prayer songs…some loud and powerful and one quiet…while his assistants tended silently to various duties around the circle.

He stopped singing and the drumming slowly came to an end. In the stillness of that moment, he spoke words that I knew in my heart were a prayer.

At the beginning of my journey on this path, the prayers seemed to have a two-fold effect on me: part sacred space, part razor-sharp attention to what was being said. As time went on and the language became clearer, I would simply drop into that sacred space and "feel" Spirit. But for some reason…in that moment…I didn't want to understand…I just wanted to "be" in that space. His words evoked a feeling in me of honor, love, respect and humility. But it wasn't just me…I could feel it in those around me. As if a silver thread connected us all.

The Intercessor's words came to an end and reluctantly I opened my eyes to see that his assistants had removed the drum. He stood there quietly while they first blindfolded him and then tied his hands behind him. Once they were finished, they helped him into a kneeling position and then placed his Eagle fan on the altar in front of him. The prayer tie fence was then closed.

Taking up the drum, his assistant began to drum a long, slow melodic beat as the people began to chant softly a prayer song. The chant went on for what seemed like forever and as I was already in a sacred place, I could immediately feel it touching my spirit. My mind spoke distantly, wanting to know the meaning of the vocals...to know what they were saying to the Creator...but my spirit just 'hushed' it. I could not say how long it was that I was in that meditative state or when I joined in with the chant for it felt as if I had always been there forever...chanting with my brothers and sisters, eyes closed, in that prayerful state. There was a sense of oneness that I had NEVER experienced and it was like water to a thirsty soul. I began to experience a sense of pressure on my ear drums and the room felt 'crowded'.

Later, I came to understand that this was when the Spirits joined the ceremony.

Eventually, the drum and singing stopped and we sat in a breathless and quiet moment…still vibrating from the chanting. I still hadn't opened my eyes because I didn't want that moment to end. I heard some quiet rustling and opened my eyes in curiosity to see that we sat in total night. I could see nothing but I continued to hear gentle rustling. In my all-consuming desire to understand the ceremonies, I had forgotten why we were here. I looked towards the area where I had last seen the young man and wondered what would come next in the ceremony for him. I could sense his mother's love and worry all the way across the room. I was unable to put myself in her place at the possibility of facing the death of her child. My thoughts touched on my only child, my daughter, and I shut that worry down immediately...worried that even considering it might actually "call" that to her.

I was shaken out of my reverie by the sound of a rattle and Dakota words being spoken, not so much in prayer as in speaking out loud to someone. I concentrated all my focus on the words spoken and became aware that though the words were being spoken by the Intercessor, they were not coming from where he sat on the rug. It sounded as if he stood before the young man 'asking' his spirits helpers something. As I sat there listening intently, a 'whoosh-whoosh' sound began to fill the room. I cocked my ear from side to side, trying to hear where it was coming from but it seemed to come from everywhere. As the 'asking' got louder and louder, so did the 'whooshing' sound. I was facing in the direction of the Intercessor's voice when all of a sudden something softly slapped across my face. The person next to me uttered a small note of surprise and I instantly recognized the feel of feathers sweeping across my face as I heard the Intercessor's voice come from across the room from me.

Now I was getting confused and my mind "needed" to make sense of it all. I had personally seen him blindfolded and his hands tied very securely. How was it that he was able to not only get out of that but get out of the prayer-tie fence without making any noise whatsoever? It couldn't have been his assistants because they had left the room. I was only half-listening to him as he appeared to be coming around the room. My logical mind demanded understanding of what was going on…and yet, a soft gentle voice in my ear was saying "be

still…'feel' the truth." I exhaled a huge sigh
and simply dropped into the faith.

At that moment, I felt a few drops of water fall
on my brow. It was so slight that it caused me
to wonder if it had actually happened and I
peered up into the darkness to see where it
came from but I could see nothing. I had the
strongest feeling that it was a kind of 'blessing'
and I bent my head in gratitude. Suddenly, the
Intercessor stood before me speaking gentle
Dakota words and brushing each side of me
ending with a final spiritual pat on the head
before moving on. Oh yes, I had definitely been
blessed.

Finally, the Intercessor spoke from the direction
of standing before the young man. In English,
he asked us to pray for the young man for
understanding of the cause of his condition and

what the spirits recommended as a healing. I heard a drum being quietly handled and a drumbeat was gently stroked from the drum as the drummer began a sing-song chant. I must have been a prayerful state all along as I was able to instantly connect with the Creator and began praying for the young one…asking for understanding of the problem his body was experiencing as well as a solution that the boy may live a long happy life. I prayed so hard and so deep that I wasn't even aware of when the ceremony ended. Suddenly, light shown thru my eyelids but it took a long time for me to come back. I heard words being spoken but it was as if I was far away observing everything down below me.

Eventually, I became more aware and opened up my eyes and took a deep yawn. The Intercessor was gone and his assistants were speaking with the boy's mother. I felt a shift in me. I had never experienced the force of 40 people <u>all praying</u> for the <u>same thing</u> at the <u>same time</u>! I looked around the room and felt such a bond of love with everyone there...realizing for the first time the true meaning of the words *Mitákuye Oyásiŋ* (We are All Related)! And I said aloud, for all to hear...

"This is what I traveled 2,000 miles for!"

6 WHAT'S IN A NAME

Most people do not know that I carry 2 names besides the one I was born with.

Asking the Intercessor at the Gathering of Elders to give me my Native name was just the beginning of a very long process. The brother who regularly poured water for our sweat lodge had developed a close relationship with Loren Zephier (now known as Golden Eagle) and he provided guidance as to what was needed for my naming such as Give-Away gifts; an idea of a name and 404 Prayer ties. I was told that the name I chose might, or might not, be the one that would be given. It would be up to the

Intercessor who would consult with the Creator and the Spirits as to my "true name".

Ah, the 404 Prayer Ties. I found this task to be the most daunting for several reasons. Once I learned how to make the Prayer ties (the trick was to use waxed string so it didn't slip), I struggled to think of a 404 different prayers. I was advised to pray for others in my life as well as other Relatives on Mother Earth.

It was a daunting task for me until I started going out into the quiet places of nature and discovered that the prayers just 'flowed' into me. At last I was able to finish all of the ties and I felt a great deal of spiritual satisfaction from performing this task. It was something I had never done before...thinking and praying for others besides family and friends...and it changed my thinking forever. I began to see how inter-connected we were. And it was the beginning of regular visits into Nature to communicate with the Creator and Mother Earth.

The gifts put me into a real quandary because the brother who was advising me could give me no idea of what to bring except to recommend cash. Instinctively, I shied away from the idea of just handing out cash. It seemed inappropriate to do so. So I kept pestering him as to what I could bring. Eventually, he let go of the idea of the cash and made suggestions such as cigarettes, towels for the sweat lodge, food, kitchen items, special sewing or craft items, and leather. As I only had 4 months to prepare, it took all my efforts to make this happen but eventually, I accumulated what I could and I felt satisfied. It would turn out however that when I presented cigarettes to the

Intercessor I found out that he did not smoke and would have preferred cash. Perhaps I should have listened but to this day, I am still uncomfortable giving cash for anything that I consider ceremony.

My family, friends and co-workers were so excited at this opportunity for me that I was inspired with a unique idea. I would have a "Naming" party where everyone could put in their ideas for my Native name. Those that could not attend emailed me their ideas. It was great fun and we laughed a lot.

A close brother from work, who I referred to as a Turtle because he was always slow to respond, gave names such as "Talks to Turtle", "Helps Turtle" or "Yells at Turtle". We all laughed so hard and I had to admit there were many appropriate and creative names.

Finally, I told everyone to pick their favorite once I left the room, to write it on a piece of paper and put it in an envelope with the Intercessor's name and to not tell me of their choice. I promised that I would carry it out to the rez and hand it to the Intercessor personally for him to 'consider' when it came time. And this I did.

When it came time for the ceremony, the Intercessor took me aside and asked me the name I had chosen and when I told him, he looked at me in surprise. Only the Creator knew the name I had chosen for I had never told anyone.

I then told him of the Naming party and I handed him the envelope. He read the name on the paper and looked genuinely shocked. I felt his attitude change towards me to one of cautious discernment. In just a few moments, our interaction had changed from one of joking around to heightened caution and I felt very uncomfortable. He told me that, except for one word, my friends had picked the exact same name.

I felt a rush of spiritual confirmation as he began to tell me of how the ceremony would happen. He told me where to sit, how I was to respond and to consider carefully the name I had chosen. The emphasis on that last statement created an immediate feeling of doubt within me…as if he was trying to "tell" me that I was making a mistake.

My Naming Ceremony was held in the same house used for the House Ceremony. The room was still empty of all furniture except one chair at the end of the room. People sat on the floor all along the walls. I was instructed to sit in the chair. I sat there nervous, trying to concentrate on the ritual to ensure that I answered correctly and at the proper time. I wanted The People to see that I showed respect to the Elders and that I knew and honored their ways. I had been taught that if I did things with a good heart and good intentions, that was all that mattered at ceremony…but I also knew that, in reality, it DID matter to get their approval.

The Intercessor came in, sat on a buffalo robe on the floor and began to start the ceremony with a prayer, I felt a 'high' that I have rarely experienced. It was one of those moments in life where a special time is frozen into your memory. Some call it a 'moment of destiny'. For me, it was so strong that the adrenaline rush was causing a headache.

Perhaps it was that 'moment of destiny' or everyone's eyes on me at the same time…but somehow, from that moment until the actual taking of the name, I totally blanked out on what was happening. I became aware and awake ONLY when I heard the Intercessor ask if I would accept my name. I hesitated for just a moment before answering. In that moment, a woman sitting next to me hissed "Don't take it…you'll regret it."

And for some reason, I didn't accept the name. I could see that I had surprised the Intercessor…surprised myself…by declining the name I had personally chosen. He and his assistants looked at each other and they quietly started brainstorming for a name. If I had my wits completely about me, I certainly would have laughed.

The 'spiritual fog' I was in started to lift the moment I was asked if I would accept Pretty Day Woman. I knew immediately it didn't fit but it didn't feel entirely wrong either. And because I felt badly for behaving like a spoiled princess…and not truly understanding why I had turned down the name I had chosen for myself…I decided in a moment to accept 'Pretty Day Woman'. But it never felt like me. I used it a few times but I never introduced myself that way in ceremonies. It never stuck. I would find out later that the name my friends and I had chosen was *Heyóka* (sometimes referred to as a 'contrary' or clown).

But this left an opening for the true name…a *Tsalagi* (Cherokee) name given in ceremony by a Cherokee Elder.

7 THE TRUE NAME REVEALED

It was at my first Vision Quest camp in Porcupine, SD, that I met a Cherokee Elder from Tulsa, OK. He had been invited by Chief Richard Swallow and we struck up a fast friendship based on the proximity of our tents to each other and our mutual interest in spiritual concepts and the Creator.

I discovered that this Cherokee Elder had made the decision to 'go on the hill' and Richard had invited him to come to Porcupine. A Vision Quest is also known as 'going on the hill'. I had no intentions of going on the hill, so I offered to help him prepare. Right before he entered the

Sweat lodge to "Become Dead to the People", he asked me to care for his eagle feather. I was shocked…and truly honored…that he would ask me to do this very sacred thing. In that moment, I stood a little higher and walked with more confidence for the Honor that was being bestowed upon me. And I realized immediately why it had been hard for me to walk with Honor and Respect. It was because I had never experienced it myself.

Looking back, I see that caring for this Elder's feather was a good lesson for me. I was so serious and conscious of my duty that I treated the feather like a child of my own. He asked me to pray with it often and I did so. I began to feel a stronger connection with Spirit. I found myself having "real conversations" with the Creator and I felt I was walking in a 'sacred space'. When the Cherokee Elder returned from the hill, I respectfully handed his feather back and thanked him for favoring me with this honor. He nodded as he received his Eagle feather and I walked away with more self-respect and self-esteem than I had ever known.

That night, as everyone was celebrating the return of the Vision Questers with a *Wophila* (Thank you) feast, the Elder shared what he could about his experiences on the hill. I was mesmerized by the stories because I could 'feel' the energy of what had happened to him. And I felt something more...I felt a sense of Humility to the Creator. I had tried several times in my life to feel real Humility but I hadn't accomplished it yet. But now, I could feel it...in the Vision Questers...in the Fire Tenders...in the Supporters who ate and drank for those on the hill, who sang for them and Prayed for them. I felt this deep, tangible sense of All of Us being in direct communication with Creator. And it felt WONDERFUL! There was such a sense of freedom and joy because I truly felt I was walking on the Red Road with the Creator.

The Elder and I talked long into the night…speaking on many things. I was in that incredible spiritual zone that I so love and I was reluctant to go bed and lose all those beautiful feelings. It was quiet and still, when this Elder quietly asked me why, if I was Cherokee, I was hanging out with Lakota. I had heard this many times before: why was a Cherokee woman following Lakota ways?

I explained to him that I had gone thru Cherokee teachings to honor my ancestors but nothing of the Cherokee ways had "called" to me. I didn't feel a connection of any kind. And

I was uncomfortable with the use of witchcraft in a spiritual tradition.

I told him that the Lakota/Dakota people had a special connection with the Creator that "drew" me. The songs filled my soul…the language "sang" to me…the ceremonies filled my heart to bursting and made me cry. Also, I liked that Lakota/Dakota ways weren't a religion but a very real way of living in harmony with All Relations. But, at the heart of it…what "called" to me was the very real connection with the Creator.

The Cherokee Elder was quiet for a bit and then he asked if I would come visit him in Tulsa. I was thrilled and honored to be asked and so I agreed that after Sun Dance out at Yankton, I would come down to visit.

That night I tossed and turned, thinking over everything I had heard, experienced and learned. When I woke up the next morning, I made the decision to go on the hill. Everyone was so kind to help me throw things together and soon I found myself kneeling in front of the Sweat lodge facing The People while Richard tied an Eagle plume to the wheel in my hair.

As we stood before The People and before the trilling of the women had died away, the Cherokee Elder stepped forward and asked for permission to speak. The Elder spoke of what I done for him, spoke of my character and that I was a Tsalagi woman…deserving of respect…and that he spoke for me and welcomed me to the Cherokee clan. And then, holding his Eagle feather high and turning to face all directions and then to the People gathered, he asked the Creator and the Spirits to hear his blessings for me. My head was bowed so no one could see the tears running down my face at his words. He stepped behind me and facing out to all the People, he spoke a *Tsalagi* Prayer and attached his feather to the medicine wheel in my hair.

2 weeks later, I stood before him in Tulsa. We had just come out of a sweat lodge at his home. He had remained inside. A short time later, he came out to stand before me and the others of his *Tiospaye* (extended family) and told me that the Creator had given him the name I would use. He said "Your new name will be Many Fires Woman." I cracked a joke along the lines of 'is that because I'll be starting fires?" He frowned disapprovingly at me and I shut up immediately. He asked me to kneel before him facing towards The People. He said that he had been shown that I would travel to many places

and speak at many council fires and that I would share things in a good way. The minute he said the name, I knew immediately it 'fit' perfectly. It was me.

Seven years later, I would learn that my last name at birth (and changed when I was 2) meant "Many Fires".

That is when I knew for certain that I was always meant to walk the path of the Red Road.

8 HAŊBLÉČHEYA
(CRYING FOR A VISION)

Traditionally one goes on their *Haŋbléčheya* (Vision Quest) only once in their life..maybe twice for special circumstances. But as one of my favorite quotes states, "I plan, Creator laughs." I shared previously in the "The True Name Revealed" my experience with the Cherokee Elder who had "gone out on the Hill." It was my experience with him, and others at the Porcupine camp, that caused me to spontaneously decide to go out on the Hill as well.

To be truthful, it was never my intention to go on the hill...ever! There were two reasons for this: I never felt the 'need' to and I didn't believe in the 'Warrior' mindset of suffering. To be fair, I heard from others how they suffered from thirst and the heat, and that most likely colored my thinking on the issue. But even if no one had spoken of these things, I saw the after-effects of being on the hill for myself - the sun burnt faces with lips so cracked they could barely speak. No, I didn't have the slightest inclination to go on my Vision Quest.

So, as you might imagine, it was a genuine surprise to me to awake that next morning and find that I had decided in my sleep that I would indeed be going up on the hill. Something...or Some One...had "called" to my soul in the night. For some reason, I kept hearing over and over in my mind the words of those who had gone up on the hill and of how the Creator had "spoken" to them. I don't think I was entirely aware of it at the time but I believe it was that 12 year old of my youth wanting to hear God "speak" to her...whispering in my mind that here was our opportunity to hear the Creator and we were going...no matter what.

And so, later that morning, I offered tobacco to a friend known as Yellow Owl, and asked him if he would put me on the hill. He agreed and we smoked his Pipe. Asking a person to put you on the hill requires a lot of trust and I trusted Yellow Owl. I knew he would truly pray for me and keep my well-being in mind the entire time I was up there. I had seen him speak and behave in an honorable way many times. After we finished, he directed me to go out and chose a place on the hill. Even though there would be 12 of us going on that hill in Porcupine...9 men and 3 women…I manage to find a lovely place under the shade of a tree near a large boulder with a beautiful view of the surrounding hills. 'Perfect', I thought to myself. I wouldn't be burned and I always did well with trees surrounding me.

20 hours later, with the chaos of getting everything ready, I sat quietly apart from the others…praying like crazy that this was going to turn out well. I kept going over and over in my mind the reasons why I had never gone on the hill.

I wasn't afraid of being attacked by wild things. That had been a huge fear at one time but I had confronted it by spending a night out on my own on my Aunt's property in the high mountains above Grass Valley. Armed with just a sleeping bag, a Navy wool blanket, some sage, a lighter and my cigarettes, I spent a night of praying, freezing and fitfully sleeping. I awoke at one point to see a large and beautiful Bob Cat, standing silently in the moonlight, looking at me sleeping in the middle of an open area encircled by trees.

Just before daybreak, I 'felt', more than heard, the sounds of something very heavy walking. Laying face down, I could feel the boom...boom...boom of each step and begged the Creator and all the *Oglígle Wakȟáŋ* (Sacred Above Beings/Angels), my Ancestors and anyone else who would listen to protect me. Somehow, I just 'knew' it was a bear even though my Aunt had never spoken about any bears. I was so scared, that my mind kept coming up with jokes. I kept envisioning the bear coming over to me and lifting one side of my sleeping bag up and saying, "Any grubs under there?" Luckily, no bear showed but later the neighbors would tell me that I was very lucky because where I had slept was right next to a long patch of berries. Truthfully, I had never thought it was luck...I felt it was the Prayers.

The second concern I had was with Spirits. Over the years, I heard things that made me feel uncomfortable. People spoke of hearing things that they felt came from the Creator...but when I heard the words spoken to them, it didn't *"feel"* like it came from the Creator. Elders told us, "there are things that mean us well, and things that do NOT mean us well. Just because one crosses over does not make that spirit a good one." The Elders said that it was not good to speak of such things too long for it would bring the wrong type of attention from the other side. And that was the reason why such things were spoken of only in ceremony…within the protection of the Creator and the Sacred Above Beings.

From that time on, I decided that I would only Pray directly to the Creator and never call on Spirit Helpers. But I worried that being in a weakened condition on the hill that I might be deceived. How would I know?

But before I could get too worried about much more, we were ushered towards the sweat lodge. The ceremony began with being presented to the people as they tied Eagle plumes into our hair (so that the Creator and Sacred Above Beings would know where we were). After that, all the Vision Questers were "dusted off" by 2 rounds in the sweat lodge and then brought out where we officially became "Dead to the People." I asked why it was that we were considered dead and was told that in the old days, many Vision Questers did not return from their vision quest. I always wondered if it was designed to fool the Trickster Spirits into leaving the Vision Questers alone.

Shortly after that, we found ourselves in a van hugging the side of the Porcupine hills, leaning precariously on a steep incline. If I hadn't been so deep into my Prayers and being 'dead', I most likely would alternately have laughed or been petrified at our 'clown car' almost tipping over and rolling down the hill. Each of us was to be placed into the spots we had chosen, where we would Pray and be guided by a Vision over the next several days.

Eventually, we came safely to the spot I had chosen. Yellow Owl directed me to lead the

Supporters (who carried everything I would have on the hill…prayer ties sleeping bag, drum, etc) to the place I had chosen. Unknown to me, it had rained early that morning and the grass was wet. Looking lovingly at the beautiful place I had chosen, I walked forward with a sense of destiny, confidence and deep reverence. Suddenly my feet slipped out from underneath me and I found myself sliding several feet down the hill. As I lay there, flat on my back, spread-eagled on the hill, looking up at the sky, it was then that I first heard the Creator laugh! A big booming laugh! I looked behind me to see that Yellow Owl and all my Supporters were looking down, desperately trying to remain serious. When they finally managed to look up without laughing, the sight of my unceremoniously sprawled body, they lost that battle and everyone began laughing so hard that we all had tears in our eyes. I laughed the hardest of all for I realized that despite my careful plans, Creator had placed me right where I had intended to avoid…out on the hill with no shade whatsoever.

They laid my sleeping bag on the grass and I stepped into an imaginary circle with my Pipe and Drum and sat down. Some of the Supporters began to tie my Prayer Flags (similar to Prayer ties) on 5 sticks and placed them around me: Yellow for the East, White for the South, Black for the West and Red for the North, with the 5th stick containing the Prayer flags of Green for Earth, Blue for the Sky and Purple for the Creator set directly before me. Others began to wrap the 404 Prayer ties around the sticks, creating a 'sacred circle' around me. Yellow Owl continued singing ceremonial songs as he placed the Sacred Foods in a bowl near the Prayer flag...*wasna*, chokecherries and buffalo fat. The sacred food was to honor the Spirits and draw them closer to hear my Prayers and carry them to the Creator or to help me in my vision quest.

After everything had been placed, Yellow Owl sang one last sweet Prayer song, said a Lakota prayer and all walked quietly away.

I settled in by arranging everything to my liking. With the laughter of the Creator still ringing in my ears...and my heart, I chuckled with sincere joy at how the Creator worked in my life. I had experienced so many of these events where one moment I was headed in one direction only to find myself going in an entirely different direction...and having it turn out right for my highest good in the end. It seemed as if I just needed to let go and let the

"River of Life" take me where I was meant to go. That night, as I fell into a sleep serenaded by crickets and the drumming and singing of the Relatives in camp sitting by the fire...I felt loved, protected and more importantly, I felt the joy of my destiny unfolding.

Many unexplained things occurred while I was on the hill. Some I can share while others I cannot. Over the days, I drummed and prayed and observed all the Relatives...for I had been told that even the smallest insect could carry a lesson from the Creator. I watched life in Porcupine circle around me. I listened to the Supporters drumming for us at night to encourage us. And I Prayed hard for a vision.

Nothing much happened that first day and night. I would find out later that the first night it rained on all the Vision Questers...except for me. The 2nd day dawned clear and fresh, heralded by meadowlarks. I felt different and I began to notice that the activity of life picked up around me. Even the winds seemed to be "speaking" to me. I prayed and sang and cried many times that day. I called on the Creator. That night I began to experience events. Shortly after sundown, as the light started to fade into black, I began to see little "lights" winking in the night. Just a few at first and then it became many. I was elated at the thought that the 'Spirits' were coming to me. The lights were so delicate and beautiful that I laughed out loud with joy. Eventually, I settled down and asked what message did they bring but they never answered…and eventually, they disappeared…leaving me once again in my solitude with the Creator…but filled with a quiet joy. I was so excited when I shared my story with the other Vision Questers in the lodge about the Spirits coming to me. Many looked at each other, then back at me and then just busted out laughing. Being a California girl, I had never seen Fireflies…and that was apparently what I had seen. We all had a good hard laugh and it was good.

Eventually I dozed off, only to awaken to an old twin-engine plane going overhead in the dark, its faint lights blinking sporadically. The minute I saw it, I remembered that my entire time on Porcupine, I had never seen a plane going over. I noticed that it was flying pretty low so I thought it might be a crop duster of some kind and by the sound of the engine, it was old.

I started to turn my attention elsewhere when something caught my eye near the tail of the plane. Following very close behind that old plane was a black shape. It had the same light configuration and the lights blinked on and off in time with the lead plane. However, it wasn't the same shape and the oddest thing is it made absolutely no sound whatsoever! Its silence was perfect. And I knew immediately it was a UFO. I chuckled to myself that I had to come hundreds of miles away from home to see my first UFO.

Later, when I began to tell of this experience in the lodge with the other Vision Questers, all the men began to snicker but the other 2 women began finishing my sentences. Of the 12 people on the hill that night, only the women saw the UFO and described it in the exact same detail.

After speaking with the Creator about the UFOs and other things I had experienced, I was finally able to settle down and I lay down to sleep. Sometime later in the night, I awoke to someone standing at my head with an extremely bright lantern shining into my eyes. Yellow Owl had told us he would come each night to check on all of us and had done so the first night. So I was not surprised to see him standing there. "Yellow Owl", I said, "that light is hurting my eyes." But the light didn't move and he didn't say a word. Remembering that I was "Dead to The People, I assumed that was the reason he did not speak. I thanked him for checking on me and laid my head back down and suddenly the light was gone. I lifted my head but didn't see or hear him walk away. I didn't think too much about it at the time as I just wanted to go back to sleep.

Afterwards, in the lodge with the other Vision Questers, Yellow Owl told me that he had gotten sick that night and never checked on any of us. And the other Vision Questers confirmed that they saw no one with a bright lantern that night. I even went so far as to question others in the camp as to whether they might have checked on me in the night. Several gave me keen looks when I asked but said nothing, except to say that it had not been them.

The last morning of my time on the hill, right before waking, I had a Vision…but it wasn't what I expected. I never understood what the vision meant and the Interpreter was unable to make sense of it. It was so alien and 'not of this Earth' that, while it does come to mind over the years, I don't give it much thought anymore. But it would not be the last time that I would be given visions/dreams of being from another place.

While I was disappointed that I hadn't received a traditional Vision to guide me thru this life, I walked away feeling as if I had been given a magical gift. I never suffered...or felt fear...not once. In fact, my Vision Quest was truly a time of beauty, connection and inspiration...with great moments of joy and laughter. I was grateful to have given away my fears in deciding to participate in this moving and uplifting ceremony. I spent time with the Creator not only in reverent Prayer but as a good friend and wise Elder. I learned the stillness of just "being", what's called 'being present. I felt the very real presence of Mother Earth and the one-ness of All Our Relations. And for the very first time, I knew...I KNEW...that I was heard, guided and honored as a Beloved Daughter of the Creator.

9 THE LODGE OF VISIONS

I have been in many sweat lodges over the years, with each one a teaching in some form from Spirit. One lodge, occurring in the beginning of my journey on the Red Road, stands out as a pivotal point in my spiritual life. I was invited to participate in a Healing Lodge to offer prayers for a beloved local Elder who had been shot in the back. This Elder meant much to me as the first time I met him, the voice of my Grandmother spoke thru his voice. Since I was new then to the ways, these kinds of events often produced a sense of confusion and yet, made me feel the Creator was truly guiding me.

This Healing Lodge was a first for many of us. We were told that the back of the lodge would be the hottest but that if any needed healing, then they should sit there. I had come not only to offer prayers for our Elder but for a dear friend who suffered a great despair and took a medication that made his spirit feel 'dead'. With a deep feeling of surrender, I made the decision to sit in the hottest part of the lodge to Pray for these two people. As I got down on my knees to crawl into the lodge, I struggled to overcome my fears.

As they brought in the first 7 rocks and the heat swelled as a great wave towards me, a feeling of deep humility filled me. I did not fight it but let it freely flow in, around and thru me. I was here to pray for my brothers. We started to sing the song of gratitude for these rocks, who were sacrificing their lives for us that we could draw even closer to the Creator and Pray in a good way. The *Ikčé Wičháša* (Common Man) pouring the lodge, asked us to breathe deep this 'breath of the Creator'...to purify our bodies, our minds, our hearts, our spirits. With each splash of the *Mní Wičhóni* (Water of Life), the rocks 'spoke' to me and the heat grew. I drew in the hot steam and immediately my lungs rebelled...coughing out the contamination of this world. Distantly, I heard the drum of the 4 songs being called...but I could not rouse myself from the darkness. And then came the call in unison: "Ho, *Mitákuye Oyásiŋ*!" And the door to the sweat lodge flew open to cool air flowing into the lodge.

As we lay on the lodge floor, gulping in the cool air, our brother spoke of the reason for this Healing Lodge. He said that in the second round, we would offer up our prayers to the Creator. He asked us to be clear and to speak with faith. Everyone was silent as the Fire Tender brought in the next 7 rocks. When all the rocks were in, the leader touched the pail of water to the rocks.

The flap to lodge fell and almost immediately, I dropped deep into my Prayers. I spoke my words into the darkness and was dimly aware that my brothers and sisters did the same. I asked for Healing for this Elder who had helped many struggling within the grasp of alcohol and for my brother-friend whose sorrow robbed him of living a life with joy. Selfishly, I spoke of how important they were in my life and I asked the Creator to bring them back into perfect balance. I was so deep in my Prayers for others that I barely noticed how intensely the heat had been building. Finishing my Prayers, I became aware of how intense the heat had become and I had to cover my head and face with my towel just to be able to breathe. I struggled to stay within that sacred place but I had never felt it this hot before and wondered if I could make it.

And then I remembered the old Grandfather from my first sweat lodge leaning over to whisper in my ear to pray even harder when it got hot…and when I could no longer take it, to lay on Mother Earth keep me cool. And so, I lay down and asked Mother to sustain me so that I might pray for my brothers. And so I managed to join in with the sacred songs and to cry out with the others, *"Ho Mitákuye Oyásiŋ!"*

Even though the flap flew open immediately, the back of the lodge held the heat longer. I was so grateful when the cool air finally brought relief. I looked around to see that all were laying on the ground, recovering.

As we lay on the ground, grasping for breath, the leader slowly spoke of our sacrifice for this Elder and for all the others for whom we had offered Prayers. Through the small light of the outside fire, I saw him dip the gourd into the water and slowly let it flow back into the pail. He did this over and over until all I could hear was the gurgle of the water... like a small stream traveling over rocks.

It was in that moment that I realized how important water was...how all Relatives upon the planet needed it to survive...how I needed it. As if knowing my thoughts, he dipped the gourd into the water and started to offer it to everyone in the lodge. As he did this, he said that the next round would be a time of listening to the answers to our Prayers. He said we had asked in faith and now we would hear the answers. He reminded us that the answers might not be what we expected but that we needed to be open to whatever came. After everyone had drunk their fill and many had sat up, he called for the flap to be closed.

The dark of the lodge was filled with anticipation. I opened up my heart and cleared my mind, intent on "hearing" the Creator speak to me. I quickly dropped into a meditative state and felt a sense of being distant from my body. I drifted further and further away until it seemed as if I was alone in the lodge. I heard the distant singing of the others but they seemed like ghosts joining me in the lodge.

Suddenly, the Elder's face came into my mind and I heard a Voice say to me "stop your Praying…he chose this…it was meant to be…he hasn't decided whether to stay or not." I was surprised and a bit troubled at being told to stop Praying but I accepted it.

More time passed. I do not know how long. I heard the 'ghosts' singing as I waited with open heart and mind. My friend's face came into my mind and I saw us laughing and playing in the water at the beach. I did not hear a voice but I was 'told' that he and I had been together before, as brothers and as priests, and that that was why I had always felt a strong spiritual connection to him. I was told to keep sharing the spiritual ways with him and that he would eventually be well. This gave me happiness and a sense of relief.

Thinking that my Prayers had been answered, I started to "return". The songs that the 'ghosts' were singing "called" to me, but instead of returning to my body, I found myself going even further away. It was then that a "slideshow' of people from different times in history came into my mind. Some were men...some were women. All seemed to be in positions of spiritual authority. As the pictures flew by, I became confused as to who these people were and why I was being shown them.

Almost as if in answer to my confusion, the slideshow came to a stop upon one man. He had shoulder-length blondish hair and was wearing a long cloak with thick fur along the shoulders. He stood at the left side of a powerful dark-haired man who had a beard and mustache. The blonde man was leaning in and quietly speaking words into the dark-haired man's ear.

Immediately, I became aware of 3 things: 1.)
that the blonde man was giving spiritual
counsel to the other one; 2) that the dark-haired
man was extremely powerful and not a good
person; and finally, 3) that all of the people in
the slideshow were me…including the blonde
man!

Instantly, I was back in the lodge, listening to
the others singing a song to the backdrop of a
drum. A feeling of shock and awe came over
me and I struggled to understand what had
happened. The intense heat brought me back
and gasping, I lay on the ground and shut my
eyes. The next thing I knew, the flap was open
and cool air was circling around us. I felt
invigorated, encouraged and blessed. And so it
was in the 4th round when the songs were called
that I joined in…with faith…with joy! While it
concerned me that I had served a dark lord in

one lifetime…I was strengthened to know that that I had always followed a spiritual path, in one form or another, thru most of my lives on Mother Earth.

10 WIWÁƞYAƞG WAČHÍPI (SUN DANCE)

I had driven late into the night when I came onto the Yankton rez and so it wouldn't be until early the next morning that I would see the pristine beauty of the place I would spend the next 4 days praying and dancing.

The next morning, I awoke early, eager with anticipation of the Sun Dance ceremony. Having been given directions the night before, I drove slowly along the small winding road to the campgrounds wondering if I would get lost and thinking of the myriad of details of setting up my campsite for the next week. I slowly became aware that there were no other cars on

112

the road and not a soul appeared at any of the distant houses. I was alone in this sacred world. I had been so engrossed in following directions that I hadn't even noticed the early morning quiet until it finally managed to 'sink' into my consciousness. The awe of that moment surrounded me...filled me...moved me. I was finally living out one of greatest dreams of my life. Feeling the significance of that moment, I let the truck slowly roll to a stop and turned the engine off.

It was then I heard...both with my ears and with my spirit...the sound of the tall grasses waving like an ocean on the prairie and the clear, pure call of a meadowlark announcing morning across the prairie. To this day, those 2 sounds can still bring me back to that moment of pure serenity, peace, and destiny.

I got out of the truck slowly and just stood in the middle of road, breathing in everything around me. It was as if I had just entered a church. My mind stilled and I felt Sacredness flowing all around and thru me. My spirit stirred. The Creator was truly there, calling to the deepest part of my soul. I instinctively knew that the wind carried the breath of the Creator and could be heard blowing thru the grasses and the trees…that it breathed Life into all of us and of the Relatives who shared Turtle Island (North America) with us. It is said that there are moments in life that are destined to happen…to fulfill us…surely this moment was one of mine. For from that time on, I not only heard the 'call' of Spirit strongly, I listened and I followed.

The heat of sun interrupted my thoughts to remind me that I needed to get my camp set up.

And as I headed down the road into the Sun Dance grounds, I thought about my reason for coming to this strange and beautiful place. Here in this place by the Missouri river, I would begin a new chapter of my life with my new name. I had been told that sometimes Naming ceremonies were performed during the Sun Dance but it had been decided that my Naming ceremony would take place right before Sun Dance and right after the House Ceremony. At that time, I had no clue what a House Ceremony was but I was spiritually hungry and felt excited to be invited to attend both ceremonies.

Setting up my tent, I had to admit I was more than a little nervous of the mistakes I might make. It had been impressed upon me before I left San Diego that the Sun Dance ceremony was special. I was told it determined what would occur in the coming year for everyone! And even though I would struggle and resist against what I thought were unfair rules, my outraged righteousness 'burned off' in the sacred flames of my first Sun Dance...leaving only a purity of spirit. It was there, in Yankton, that I began to truly understand what it meant to walk The Red Road.

Once I finished setting up my campsite, I went to look at Sun Dance grounds. I could see from a distance that the center of the Sun Dance arbor had a forked cottonwood tree with Prayer Flags and Ties hanging in the branches along with necklaces, eagle feathers, representations of the White Buffalo and other sacred items. As I got closer, I could see a long bundle crossing the fork in the tree horizontally and creating a kind of 'spiritual bridge'. A buffalo skull sat at the foot of the tree and wooden posts, crowned with tree branches surrounded the entire arbor to provide shade to the Supporters. I had been told the night before that I would also be a 'Supporter' for the Sun Dance. Supporters danced, sang and prayed for the entire 4 days in support of the Dancers.

Standing there, looking up at the tree, I remembered what had been shared with us back home about the Sun Dance. It was called "The People's ceremony" and was for ALL nations. It was considered one of most sacred of all Lakota/Dakota ceremonies and I remember likening it to the High Holy days of the Jewish tradition. In "Black Elk Speaks", Black Elk shares a vision of all Nations...all Colors...joining together in ceremony. He said that when this happened, it would be the beginning of a "Mending of the Hoop" for the world...when the world would once again become balanced and there would harmony between all Nations. There was always talk of hope for that day when a member of All Nations would Sun Dance for the good of The People.

A Sun Dancer usually pledged to dance for 4 years at a specific Dance. They danced for a variety of reasons...to ask for a healing for a family member or a friend...to ask for help for someone or to give thanks to the Creator for a healing or help from the previous year. The most sacred reason to dance was to Pray for the welfare of The People. The Dancers fulfilled their vows by dancing for 4 days in the hot sun with no food or water, keeping their gaze on the sun (or in some dances, on the top of the sacred tree) the entire time.

Occasionally, a male dancer would 'pierce' (women do not pierce) on the 3rd or 4th day. The act of piercing is a ritual performed by a medicine man. He will pinch together a fold of loose skin from the breast and run a very narrow-bladed sharp knife through the skin underneath. Then, a skewer of bone, about the size of pencil, would be inserted. The bone was then attached to a long rope that would be attached to the top of the Sun Dance tree. Over the course of the 2 days, the dancer would slowly break loose by pulling away from the tree and tearing the skewers out. This was considered a "flesh offering". Women Sun Dancers could give flesh offerings by having a small piece of skin cut from their upper arm with a razor.

Sitting on log by the sacred fire watching the rocks heat for the evening sweatlodges, I could see the Women Sun Dancers carry their bundles into the tipi they would sleep for the next 3 nights. For them, this was the beginning of a very sacred time. Being a Sun Dancer was considered to be a Sacred Honor and during the 4 days, they were considered to be Holy. As one of the women bent down to go into the tipi, she saw me looking at her and gave me a smile of welcome. I gratefully smiled back and sat there wondering if I could ever have the courage to be a Sun Dancer.

Later that evening, after everyone had finished setting up their camps, all were asked to attend an Sweat lodge to clean off the 'stinking thinking' of the outside world. After the non-stop 21 hour drive, the Sweat lodge revealed the depth of my exhaustion and I passed up the opportunity to sit by the fire and make new friends. Settling snugly into my sleeping bag, I had no time to review the day as I fell quickly into a deep sleep.

The 1st day of Sun Dance, I awoke to the camp crier yelling across the camp just before sunrise: "Hoka Hey! It is a good day!" I dressed quickly in a long skirt and shirt and after my morning routine, made my way to the camp kitchen for some coffee and some good conversation over breakfast. One of the things I liked best when attending Sun Dances were the variety of people from different places and sometimes different lands. Over the course of the previous 2 days, I had observed Sun Dancers putting finishing touches on their dress/skirts or moccasins. The women wore simple dresses they made themselves and men wore skirts – both had to be of 100% cotton. Often you would see a Dancer start to hum a sacred song or walk away if a negative or unkind word was being said. Then there were the experienced ones who had done this so many times and knew exactly what was expected of them. Some were kind and helpful towards the newcomers, others would display disdain for not knowing the right thing to do. But it was the spiritual conversations with the people who had heard the 'call', as I had, who had experienced 'supernatural' events but didn't know what it all meant that drew me the most. Those spiritual conversations nourished my soul.

Finally, as the sun rose fully over the hills, the drums started and that was the signal that for the Sun Dancers to enter the arbor and start the Dance. I was nervous and reluctant to leave the safety of the camp kitchen. Eventually, I made my way slowly to where I had placed my camp chair the day before to save a place. I knew no one around me and I felt as if the people around me looked on me as an interloper. Eventually, my self-consciousness left me and I watched as the Intercessor (Sun Dance leader) and his helpers entered the arbor and guided the Sun Dancers to the Eastern Gate, which faced the rising sun. The drums held a slow beat. There was a certain solemn majesty to the Dancers as the helpers guided them slowly to the spot they would begin this Sun Dance...and in the end, they would return. Eventually, all were in place. The dancers held Eagle or Red Tail Hawk fans in their left hands and wore bands of woven sage around their brows, wrists and ankles. Sometimes they wore paint on their face or red clay for protection from the sun. Some held Eagle whistles in their mouths. All looked up towards the rising of the sun, lifting one foot and then the other as the beat of the drums began to grow in strength.

The drums grew louder and stronger as the sun rose, I felt something deep awaken within me and I felt *different*. Over the next 4 hours of dancing, singing and praying, I began to feel something take hold of my spirit, my soul...something greater than myself. I began to 'know' that I was more than the personality I had worn as a cloak all my life. My neighbors and I looked at each other, exhausted, and smiled with joy for we realized that we were all the Sons and Daughters of the Creator and for the first time, we were as One.

Around noon the Dancers were given a break and the Supporters headed to the camp kitchen for lunch. It was considered our sacred duty to eat and drink for the Sun Dancer so that it would ease their hunger and thirst and keep them focused on their Prayers. As the day wore on, we all became tired, hot and thirsty. From my vantage point in the shade of the arbor, I watched the Sun Dancers with growing respect and admiration. Could I ever go without food and water and dance in the hot sun for 4 days? As the sun started to go down, the Intercessor and his Helpers guided the Dancers to their tipis to rest for the night.

I walked slowly back to my camp to change clothes before heading to the kitchen for dinner. I was tired but energized at the same time. I was living out one of my life's dreams but there was something more happening. I could genuinely '*feel*' this deeper connection to the Creator. It was as if the Creator was answering that 12-year olds prayer...the Creator was 'talking' to me!

That night I sat with the Fire Tenders who were tending the sacred fire. We talked long into the night in a companionable way. We drank coffee, shared our experiences and listened to each other's truths. We talked of the meaning of walking the Red Road…of honor, respect and doing things in a "good way". I learned some valuable things that night around the fire but 2 stand out. One was serving for the good of The People…the idea being that being of service for even 1 person served Everyone. What also came to me that night was that ritual wasn't what the Creator required…all that was required was to LOVE. Yet, the wise spiritual leaders knew that the 2-leggeds needed discipline and structure…and that eventually the ritual of a ceremony would bring us closer to the Creator…close enough to 'hear' and we would be guided from there.

On the 2nd morning I awoke filled with pure JOY! I had dreamed all night and had been awakened mid-dream. 'They' had spoken to me all night and had given me so much information, yet strangely, I remembered none of it. It didn't seem to matter though for not only did I feel like I was home but that this was the beginning of huge change in my life. The only dream I did remember was being shown the face of a man who was attending the dance, and told to stay away from him...that he was not as he pretended to be. This would be the beginning of the type of real dreams in which I would be 'told', or guided, to do something that ultimately would help me or others...and would in 2 cases save my life.

I could feel the heat of the day even before I left my tent that 2nd day of Sun Dance and I was grateful to be camped under the Cottonwoods with a cool breeze from the Missouri River blowing on me. As I walked through the camp that morning, I was amazed to see a White-tail Deer calmly walk right by me thru the middle of camp. I was surprised to see the Deer was completely unafraid of all the 2-leggeds and I asked my friend about it. He told me that while he and his brothers hunted the White-tail throughout the season, that all the animals knew they were protected during the Sun Dance.

I only had time for needed coffee before hurrying down to the Arbor. Dancing slowly, I watched the Dancers entered the Arbor. I could see that they too felt the heat of the direct sun as I had that morning.

That day was the hardest, not only for the Dancers but for the Intercessor, the Helpers and the Supporters as well. Throughout the day, some of the Dancers experienced heat exhaustion and were attended to. I felt such compassion and respect for them and it made me want to dance and pray harder. I understood that they were sacrificing and that this was needed...for the good of All...but it did not stop my woman's heart from wanting to help them.

The morning round finally came to an end and many of us were so happy to see the Dancers given the opportunity to rest in the shade. Many of us just simply collapsed in our chairs for awhile, getting up only to drink water, out of sight of the Dancers. It was too hot to eat, so I sat there in my chair watching the Helpers ease the Dancers discomfort and thinking again about the significance of sacrifice.

I was never one to sacrifice. Oh I could make small gestures such as helping people with food, a ride, small loans and always lend an ear to listen when someone needed to talk. But I never had been one for physical sacrifice. It had just never felt necessary.

Sitting there, watching the Dancers struggle with their sacrifice and experiencing my own struggle with the heat...many thoughts came and went in my mind. For some reason a memory of something I had learned from my Religious Studies classes. It was a theory put forth by Jewish scholars that the Native American tribes might be the lost 12th tribe of Judea. I remembered thinking that I thought it might be possible because of a story a Lakota Elder had shared with me. He told me that long ago, the people used to sacrifice by giving up their lives to help a loved one or friend or to help The People suffering from a tremendous hardship. Many times (but not always) these were young men and during one particularly hard winter, many of the young men took their lives, leaving The People with very few young men to hunt for food. The Elders came together and prayed to the Creator to ask what could be done. They wanted to honor their young people's desire to serve The People but in doing so it might cause The People to starve. One night, the Spiritual Leader had a dream in which he was told to tell the People they must sacrifice an animal made sacred instead of sacrificing their own lives in order that the People might live. This is how I was told that *Šúŋka* (dog) stew came to be a part of ceremonies. To me, this seemed very similar to the Jewish tradition of sacrificing a Lamb for ceremonies.

The afternoon session began and a cooler breeze seemed to blow in the arbor. The Dancers, even with the rest, were struggling to keep their energy up in the heat. As I danced in the spot worn down by my feet for 2 days, I looked upon their suffering and felt humility grow within. Despite my own exhaustion, I danced and prayed even harder, focusing all my energy on supporting the Dancers. I began praying in earnest for Everyone I knew...all that had asked for prayers...and even those who hadn't. I asked the Creator to help the Dancers and all the Supporters for I could see that many of us were struggling and needed help. I prayed as I had never Prayed before...and the tears flowed down my face and dropped into rivulets on my dusty feet. My heart cried out to the Creator and I wept, unashamed. Someone placed a tender comforting hand on my shoulder in compassionate understanding.

I do not know how long it was that I prayed that way. At long last, my Prayers came to an end and I looked up to the sky above the arbor to thank the Creator...and that is when I had my first vision...ever.

Circled around the arbor in the sky above were the Ancestors of past days. There were men and women dressed in traditional buckskin and they too were dancing to the beat of the drum and smiling down at me...at Us! I could "feel" their approval and joy radiate out towards all there. A rush of adrenaline and excitement filled me and I looked at my neighbors wanting to grab their arms and say 'Look! Look! The Ancestors are here!' But I stopped short, thinking they might laugh at me. And that moment of doubt made me wonder if I had truly seen the Ancestors. What if it had been the heat and the thirst? What if it was what my mind wanted to see.

With the innocence of a child, I wanted to see those smiling angelic faces of approval and so I shyly look to the skies again. What I saw next made me understand how important it was what we are were doing there.

I saw that the circle of Ancestors was widening and deepening. More and more Ancestors were joining the circle and what was even more amazing was that they were Ancestors from All Races. They were dressed in different clothes for each culture...some in modern dress...many in ancient attire. They kept coming until the Circle filled the sky...and yet I could sense that even more kept coming...filling the skies about the arbor in sacred dance.

I wept openly and my tears of Joy did not stop. The time for Praying was over and I was simply deeply and humbly grateful for this sign. The Ancestors were there for only a short time and eventually they disappeared as a rainbow might. At the end of the afternoon session, I quietly left for my camp and did not return.

I did not sit with the Fire Tenders that night or visit with others after dinner. Instead, I sat at my campsite thinking over everything I had experienced that day. I wondered if anyone else had seen the Ancestors. Every time I thought of the vision, I smiled thinking not only did I get to see my very first vision but I got to see that there truly were Ancestors and how important the Sun Dance was. I thought of my small worries and complaints and saw with clarity just how unimportant they were.

That night as I tried to sleep, the vision kept coming into sight and I began to realize that my Spirit had been 'shifted' into another way of being...of thinking...that day. And I knew I would never be the same.

The 3rd day I awoke, after a long night of dreams, to someone saying outside my tent. "*Hoka hey*! It is a good day to die!" I remember hearing that statement years before and thinking I didn't care for it because of the 'doom and gloom' feeling to it. It was then that a brother, Yellow Owl, explained that the Creator had given each of us everything we needed...our health, our families, good food, clean water, and the ceremonies...so each day we were alive, we should be prepared to die with gratitude and no regrets. I liked that. And after what I had experienced the day before, I felt I could indeed die with gratitude and no regrets.

Some friends joined me in the walk to the kitchen that morning. The 3rd day, they told me, was considered a day of Healing and Laughter. In the early afternoon, the Sun Dancers were lined up in front of the Supporters opposite them. Each Dancer approached every Supporter in line either greeting them with quiet words of blessings or prayers… brushing them off with their Eagle/Hawk fans. Sometimes a Dancer would seem to know a vulnerable place in the body and pat them there with their fan…all the while rocking back and forth on their heels and singing a Sun Dance song. Others lifted their faces to the sky and offered prayers to the Creator over them. This was seen as a sacred event. Having a Dancer pray for you or place their healing touch upon you was considered a direct blessing from the Creator…for the Dancers were in a Sacred place. I saw several people who were healed on that 3rd day but 2 memories stand out: A man got up out of his wheelchair carefully walked across the arbor to hug his son and a woman was healed of cervical cancer. People responded with cries of amazement, with thanks to the Creator and with tears of gratitude.

While those same tears of gratitude and joy were still on many of our faces, a Clown suddenly appeared, dancing in the arbor. His face was painted with black and white stripes and he was wearing underpants on his head. A shirt was wrapped around him like a skirt and instead of a crown of sage like the Dancers wore; his crown was made of weeds. He proceeded to tease the Dancers by throwing water on them or letting the water slowly fall into the dirt right in front of them. He juggled fresh fruit in front of them and ate cold watermelon with the juice running down his stomach. He squirted the Supporters with squirt guns and juggled for the children...throwing them candy and fruit. The People started to laugh. And so it was that amongst the Tears of The People, came the Laughter of The People as well. I too laughed thru my tears...and it felt good. I did not need to be told what this all meant. I knew this was a Life's teaching... that no matter how hard our trials in life were, The People could still laugh with joy and be grateful for all they had in life. And I felt in my heart what it meant for it to be a "good day to die."

There were many uplifting conversations floating in the summer air that night. I finally felt like I was exactly where I was supposed to be and just KNEW Creator had brought me to this place. I could genuinely feel the oneness of "*Mitákuye Oyásiŋ*" (We are All Related). Everyone was talking and laughing and filled with hope. And as I spoke deep and long with the Creator that night, tears of joy fell like a spring shower. And the dreams that came were powerful and prophetic.

When I finally awoke the morning of the 4th day, I was filled with the kind of hope and wholeness that fills the soul. Yet a sense of prophecy clung to me…asking for my attention but I was too excited about the day's events to be deterred by any other distracting thoughts. Today was the last day of Sun Dance and I wanted to fill up with every moment of spiritual nourishment I could to take home with me. Today was going to be a wonderful day!

The 4th day of the Sun Dance was a time for a huge *Wophila* (Thank you) feast for everyone afterwards. You could see the happiness on the faces of the Sun Dancers as they entered the arbor that morning. I noticed right away that they walked with a greater dignity. And, for having danced 3 days in the hot sun with no food or water, I was genuinely surprised to see such energy in their steps. Even the birds seemed to sing them their highest praise with songs of joy as the great sun rose in the East.

The anticipation of the end of the Sun Dance ceremony was palpable that morning. Supporters came and went with great smiles on their faces. Women were eagerly chatting with each other in the kitchen while the children laughingly chased each other throughout the camp. The aroma of seared meat floated over all...making it difficult to concentrate on anything but the growling in our stomachs. Even the drummers, who had many times lost their voices over the course of the 4 days, sang out pure, clear and strong...filling the Dancers with a reborn strength to dance with ever lighter and higher steps. And as I danced with them that morning, thanking the Creator for opportunity to be there in that moment, I was pretty sure that the minds of many a Dancers, was on the best part of the meal that was always served first...cold, sweet watermelon!

In the afternoon, there came a final Pipe Ceremony. All through the 4 days, designated Dancers would step forward and offer up their Pipes to the Supporters to smoke and send forth Prayers. This was a great honor and the Family/Supporters made sure to smoke the Pipe of their favorite Dancer. There was always a lot of noise in the background as people sat down and chatted with each other. Often, the Sun Dance leader would ask the Supporters for their silence and to show respect for the Pipe.

But on this day, there was no need. No one sat down. No one talked. All stood in respectful silence and stillness to honor this sacred ceremony. As the Pipe Ceremony ended, the Dancers returned to the arbor. The drummers began a slow drumbeat and the Dancers began the last dance of the Sun Dance Ceremony with a sacred, almost regal, reverence. As the round continued, the Dancers danced to all 4 Directions to acknowledge and honor all Relations. And finally, back to the Tree. Once the Dancers were back in their original places in which they started, the drums and the Dancers stopped together. The Sun Dance leader spoke a Prayer of Gratitude and Humility and afterward led the Dancers out of the arbor to participate in one last sweat lodge in which the Dancers would share, and hear, the interpretations of their visions.

Afterwards, the Dancers would clean up and join everyone in the kitchen area where they were brought watermelon and the best of all the foods that had been cooked. Everyone would eat until they were more than satisfied. Afterwards, there were games and Giveaways and testimonials…all of which lasted until sundown. Giveaways were always fun. These were gifts given away either in honoring a momentous event in their family's life or in memory of someone who had "walked on". Some gifts were given to specific people while others were handed out to The People as a whole. The gifts could be money, blankets, towels, kitchen items, candy or tobacco.

I walked away from the *Wophila* feast, having had my fill, and packed up my campsite. By the time, I decided to make one last round to say goodbye to those who were still there, it was dark. The hugs, the laughter, the promises to see each other next year filled my heart and completed something in me. I had found a spiritual community that nourished me and I belonged with them. Just before leaving, I stood for one last look at the Missouri River and felt the change within me from when I came 4 days ago. This was a sacred place and I needed to return.

Just as everyone started to completely leave the grounds, the winds started to blow ferociously but no rains came. I decided that instead of staying over at my hosts' home for one last night, that perhaps it would be wise to start the long drive home right then. I had a lot on my mind and heart that I needed to think on and that long road in front me promised a thoughtful ride with many 'talks' with the Creator.

As I drove out the small road for the last time, lightning began to flash and had started building to major bolts that dominated the sky. Like most native San Diegans, I am utterly enamored of major storms... especially lightning...and I drove slowly to see all I could. I began to notice that the lightning appeared to have a color to it. I shook my head to clear my eyesight because I was definitely seeing PINK lightning (yes, I said Pink)! The lightning, like the wind, became fierce, with lightning strikes starting to touch down to the ground on my left. I started to get that odd 'tingle' of intuition telling me this was not entirely random. I called out aloud to the storm, "Creator, should I stay or should I leave now?" As if in direct response to my question…and I swear this happened…a massive bolt of Pink Lightning immediately struck the middle of the road literally in front of the truck! I slammed on the brakes and yelled out to the ether, "I think I'll stay tonight then." Immediately, the lightning stopped!

I was so amazed at how quick the responses had come at Yankton. It seemed as if the Creator was 'talking' to me…guiding me along my path…strengthening that connection. And the Sun Dance? Well, it cleared the pathways so I could clearly 'hear' the Creator…making me more of a 'Hollow Bone' as Frank Fools Crow would have said.

From that time on, Yankton always held a special place in my heart. I would go to many beautiful places and attended many Sun Dances over the years but it is Yankton that 'sings' to me. Those memories of the tall grass, a meadowlark in the perfect silence of an early morning, the shadow of trees against the background of the Missouri River and the smoke of the campfires in the early morning call to me from across the years. The heartbeat of the drums as the puffs of dust from a dancer's moccasins flying before the winds of a prairie storm play in slow motion in my mind's eye. I remember the hard lesson of 'gifting' something precious and dear to an Elder. And most especially, I will never forget that it was at Yankton where I received my first Vision of the Ancestors from All Nations.

All of those memories "call" out to me across the years to 'come home'. For 4 days, I prayed, danced and breathed in Honor, Humility,

Generosity and Sacrifice and saw the Ancestors watching us in approval of what we did there. After living those 4 days in a "good way", I left the Yankton Sun Dance a completely changed and better Human Being…and I began to like who I was becoming.

11 BECOMING MY TRUE SELF

"The Red Road ain't for sissies!" I was caught off guard by the brother's firm statement as he sat with his eyes focused distantly on the horizon. He had been silent up to that point as I had 'whined' about the many things I found archaic and impossible in these ways. I stopped mid sentence, hurt at the insinuation that I was a sissy. I felt like a scolded child. I started to come back with a smart comment but the sting of tears in my eyes caught me by surprise and I kept silent.

The brother dropped his eyes to the ground and continued, "I felt the same way as you growing up in these ways. I lived with my Auntie and Uncle and I resented them for insisting that I go to the Ceremonies. I thought Auntie and Uncle were old-fashioned and out of touch with the real world. I only wanted to hang out with my friends and have fun. As I grew older, that 'fun' turned into more serious things and eventually I found myself in prison. It was then I came face to face with who I really was. A lot of guys get religion in prison, and I did too. It was a way of trying to understand how we came to end up in a place like that…and it was a way to take your mind off where you were. There was this Navajo man who used to come to the prison once a month and pour water for a lodge. I had nothing to do, so I decided to go. His teachings reminded me of the Ceremonies I had attended as a child but more than that…they made me think of my Grandfather. He used to take me out into nature and show me how the world worked…and our role in it. He taught me that the Ceremonies not only connected our heads to our hearts…but kept us connected to the Creator..for that was the true Red Road."

When I began searching for a title to my story, my *hunka* (adopted) brother asked me a pivotal question: "why are you writing this book?"

I thought on his question for a long time. In the beginning, it had started out as a record of my journey in these ways…maybe a bit of biography for my family…opening that part of my life that they had laughed at in the beginning but eventually grew to respect. I wanted them to know that part of me I held Sacred.

But as I began to write the stories, I found my thoughts turning more and more towards the

Ceremonies. Perhaps it was Frank Fools Crow 'speaking' to me...telling me how important it was to share the Ceremonies when he said: *"Survival of the world depends on our sharing what we have learned, and working together. If we do not, the whole world will die. First the planet, and next the people. "*

Suddenly, I wanted...***needed***...to share how living the Ceremonies had caused me to look at Life...ALL Life...in a new and different way. Perhaps, I thought to myself, the Creator wanted me to share the true value of the Ceremonies, and the Red Road, and to share what a difference they had made in my life.

The spiritual ways of the Lakota/Dakota people had 'called' to me to me in my teen years. I had felt a kinship with the Sacredness they held for this world and to the Creator. I read the words of their Leaders and they were strong and true and full of wisdom. And I knew even then that I wanted to live in a world filled with those words.

That 'Call' never stopped until it found me in 1986. However, it wouldn't be until I walked into my first Ceremony that I would begin to really feel what it meant to be a Cherished Daughter of the Creator. Each Ceremony I attended seemed to bring not only healing to those wounded places in me but "watered" the garden of my faith and brought a spiritual sustenance that would ripple out to all parts of my life and extend to those around me.

And even though I gained great pleasure thru my travels to many places sitting at 'many fires' and speaking with new friends, it was the

Ceremonies of the Red Road that inspired and changed me.

Through them, I began to truly understand that we were indeed related to each and every Relative on the planet. I learned that Mother Earth was a loving, sentient being and that we were Her caretakers. I learned to sacrifice for the "Good of The People" with the understanding that the good done for one benefited all. I discovered how truly important it was to Pray for others…and the miracles that could happen when we did. And I came to understand that the Creator (and other unseen beings) 'talked' to us, if we would only listen.

Now, when I look back to that day when I was 12, I realize that Creator hadn't overlooked me. He was just waiting for me to learn to 'listen' through the Ceremonies...to discover that we all hear the same Voice...a voice heard by *Mitákuye Oyásin* (All My Relations).

And that is how the Ceremonies helped me become a "True Human Being".

ABOUT THE AUTHOR

Lynn Manyfires, ordained in 2010, has followed a spiritual path her entire life. Introduced to the Lakota/Dakota spiritual ways (known as the 'Red Road') 30 years ago, it was the Ceremonies that enlightened her and lifted her to a higher calling. Following the guidance of her dreams in 1996, she gave up her job, her home and her way of life to go on a spiritual quest. Traveling to reservations in 5 states, she attended Ceremonies, listened to the wisdom of the Elders and experienced the extraordinary connection that the Lakota/Dakota Nations have with the Creator and with Mother Earth. Honored to have been selected as a Pipe Carrier in the late 90's, she came to fully understand the importance of Lakota ceremonies on creating sacred Community. Lynn believes that the Ceremonies will help to re-create the healthy foundations needed for families and their communities and will restore the values that are honored by all Indigenous Peoples of the world: Respect, Honor, Bravery, Sacrafice, Generosity, Wisdom, Humility, Truth, Love, Perseverance and Compassion. She continues to honor the 'Mission Statement' given to her by the Creator to serve for the good of 'The

People' by offering community presentations that focus on these values. Lynn's faith that the Ceremonies will be the catalyst for developing a cooperative spirit in our communities has inspired her to write this book. By sharing her experiences of the Red Road, the wisdom of a sacred way of life will bring peace, balance and harmony to a world in need.

Made in the USA
Lexington, KY
16 March 2016